ACADEMIA
BARILLA

SALADS

50 Easy Recipes

CREATED BY
ACADEMIA BARILLA

PHOTOGRAPHY
ALBERTO ROSSI
CHEF LUCA ZANGA

RECIPES
CHEF MARIO GRAZIA

TEXTS
MARIAGRAZIA VILLA

DESIGN
MARINELLA DEBERNARDI

COORDINATION WITH ACADEMIA BARILLA
CHATO MORANDI
ILARIA ROSSI
REBECCA PICKRELL

CONTENTS

Salads. A Taste Sensation!   page   6
The Art of Dressing   page   11

Salads with Vegetables and Fruits   **page   14**
Orange, grapefruit and lemon salad   page   16
Asparagus salad   page   18
Avocado, orange, melon and strawberry salad   page   20
Beet salad   page   22
Cabbage salad with dried apricots and hazelnuts   page   24
Citrus-scented chickpea salad   page   26
Salad of soybean sprouts, carrots and watermelon   page   28
Fresh vegetable and corn salad   page   30
Mango salad with yellow peppers and carrots   page   32
Potato salad   page   34
Salad of celery root, radicchio and pineapple   page   36
Pink grapefruit, spinach and walnut salad   page   38
Zucchini salad with mint   page   40
Pinzimonio   page   42

Salads with Cheese and Eggs   **page   44**
Caprese salad   page   46
Greek salad   page   48
Warm goat cheese salad   page   50
Artichoke salad with Parmigiano-Reggiano   page   52
Assorted cheese salad   page   54
Pecorino salad with fava beans and Parma ham   page   56
Pear salad with gorgonzola and walnuts   page   58
Arugula salad with Parmigiano-Reggiano   page   60
Salade Niçoise   page   62

4

Salads with Meat and Fish   page 64
Condiglione   page 66
Rabbit salad with lamb's lettuce   page 68
Endive and prosciutto salad   page 70
Apple, chicken and toasted focaccia salad   page 72
Chicken salad with balsamic vinegar and pine nuts   page 74
Octopus salad with citrus fruits   page 76
Monkfish and tomato salad   page 78
Smoked salmon and fennel salad   page 80
Tuna salad with beans   page 82
Mimosa salad with trout   page 84
Veal salad with honey-sesame dressing   page 86
Mixed salad greens with speck and raspberries   page 88
Panzanella   page 90
Octopus salad with potatoes   page 92

Salads with Pasta and Grains   page 94
Grain salad with herbs and vegetables   page 96
Margherita-style pasta salad   page 98
Vegetarian couscous salad   page 100
Bowtie pasta salad with melon balls and vegetable confetti   page 102
Fusilli pasta salad with asparagus and prosciutto crudo   page 104
Sardinian-style pasta salad with tuna, zucchini and bell peppers   page 106
Mezze maniche pasta salad with prawns, cherry tomatoes and eggplant   page 108
Orecchiette pasta salad with cod, fava beans and olives   page 110
Whole-grain pasta salad with avocado, chicken, cherry tomatoes, and corn page 112
Spring rice salad   page 114
Venus rice salad with cherry tomatoes and mozzarella   page 116
Sedanini pasta salad with green apples, raisins and almonds   page 118
Warm spelt salad with scampi   page 120

Alphabetical index of recipes   page 122
Alphabetical index of ingredients   page 124

5

SALADS
A TASTE SENSATION!

"The farmer's wife brought me the mallow
and the various products growing in my garden,
the broad-leafed lettuce,
leeks to cut into slices,
fragrant mint and various herbs."
Martial, *Epigram* X, 48

Is there anything more cheerful than a nice salad filled with a wealth of enticing shapes, colors, textures and flavors? Salads can excite every sense and can be an open door to the joy and pleasure of sharing with friends and family. There is no limit to how they can bring harmony to a meal. From the simplest – lettuce from the field dressed with a drizzle of oil, a few drops of lemon and a pinch of salt – to the most elaborate and creative – small masterpieces from Renaissance banquets that combined herbs, flowers, fruits, meats, fish – everyone is fascinated by salad. And, if carefully prepared, it never falls short of expectations.

A "Savory" Origin

It all starts from a grain of salt. The term "salad" is derived from the archaic Italian word *insalare*, meaning "to add salt". But what do we mean when we speak about salad? In Italian cuisine, the word indicates a plate of vegetables, mixed or of a single type, usually raw, but which may also be cooked and served cold; the dish is dressed with salt, oil and vinegar or lemon. But it may also indicate, by extension, any cold plate that is dressed in such a manner, including dishes that do not even include vegetables, or where vegetables appear only as a flavouring or decorative element. Thus, we speak of a rice salad or pasta salad, where the basis of the dish is constituted by such grains, usually

complemented by vegetables, cheeses, legumes and various condiments, or a chicken or beef salad, where the meat is boiled and let cool, then cut into small pieces and added to other ingredients that give it flavour. There are some salads that have fish as the main ingredient, the Sicilian bottarga salad, for example, or where legumes play the starring role, as in the case of salads of beans, chickpeas, or fresh fava beans. In Italy, salad comes in many forms.

A Story for Every Herb

If, by the term "salad", we mean the consumption of fresh vegetables, dressed to a greater or lesser extent, then the history of this dish is lost in the mists of time and becomes confused with the adventure of human nutrition itself. In fact, there is no geographic or cultural area where prehistoric man, even before becoming a hunter, did not think of transforming edible wild plants into salad. Salad was found in ancient cave drawings, where we find paintings of the gathering of grasses, roots and tubers, and salad also arrives at royal tables. It would seem that cultivated lettuce had already appeared on the table of the King of Persia around 550 BC!

If this dish is ancient in Italy, we owe it to the Romans: even while being enthusiastic consumers of meat, fish, cheese and bread, they didn't neglect the produce of the vegetable garden. Nearly always dressed in a robust, spicy and pungent manner, salads of vegetables and legumes were served during their interminably long banquets, with the function of reawakening the appetite. Widespread among the Romans was the first "cheese salad", which constituted the sustenance of farmers and soldiers: this was the *moretum*, composed of mint, rue, savory, coriander, celery, leek, lettuce leaves, rocket and fresh thyme, all ground together with fresh cheese and various types of nuts, in a mortar, then dressed with salt, oil and vinegar.

After the Middle Ages, when meats triumphed on the tables of nobles, the Renaissance saw salads of vegetables come into vogue, enriched with fruits, oil seeds, flower blossoms, herbs and various bold and

unusual ingredients. Vegetables were showcased, thus, not as a food for the poor, but as pivotal ingredients of sumptuous creations; they were seen as the works of great chefs.

The Importance of Preliminaries

As far as tasting goes, salad is very easy. In the Italian language there is a saying referring to "eating someone like salad", meaning to get the better of a person with the same ease with which one would eat a salad.

However the preparation of the salad is not as simple as it may seem, and a few tricks are necessary to make sure it comes out tasty and balanced. First of all you need to choose the individual ingredients that will go into your salad with great care. To avoid having your salad turn into a confused jumble, it is a good idea, when still a beginner, to follow a recipe, then over time you can apply a few changes as personal touches if you like. It is most important to use ingredients that can combine with one another in a harmonious way, so that they compliment one another rather than compete. Furthermore, make sure to choose only the freshest vegetables and, when preparing, trim with care, eliminating the parts that are hard or ruined. Wash your vegetables carefully, taking care not to leave them in water for too long, otherwise they risk losing many of their vitamins and minerals. Dry them well, making sure to handle them gently rather than roughly (for leaf vegetables, it is better to use the kitchen cloth, held by the four corners, rather than a salad spinner). When cutting, cut them into shapes as regular as possible: into thin strips or cubes, but also little sticks, rounds or thin ribbons.

Regarding the salad bowl, it must be sufficiently deep and spacious so that you can conveniently dress the salad. The choice of materials, however, leaves room for discussion. Purists prefer wood because they consider it more appropriate for vegetables but the more practical opt for glass or ceramic, because these do not absorb fats and odors, nor do they react with vinegar. As for serving utensils, glass or bone are preferred, while metal should never be used.

When to Enjoy it

When is the best time during the meal to serve the salad? A classic salad of fresh or cooked vegetables, unquestionably, makes an excellent accompaniment or side dish for a main dish of meat or fish. If the salad, however, is of mixed ingredients, composed not only of vegetables, but also protein, such as cubes of cheese, slices of prosciutto or legumes, this can provide a tasty appetizer or it can constitute an excellent and refreshing single course meal, particularly in summer months or at midday. All sorts of special salads, containing elements that are predominantly non-vegetable, may be situated at the point of the meal suggested by their base ingredient. A salad of spelt, for example, is a first course, while a salad of boiled ingredients becomes, for all intents and purposes, a main course dish. Exceptions to this would be salads that are particularly light, such as those made with shellfish or raw meat, that are often proposed as appetizers.

From Italy to the World

The "original" salad, composed of vegetables, raw or cooked, is appreciated in all gastronomic traditions. The salad, however, finds its land of choice in Italy, where farming culture and the economy of the vegetable garden have roots dating back thousands of years: Italian cuisine – through its gradual welcoming of various items of vegetable produce of Asian origin, such as the eggplant and the artichoke or of American origin, such as the potato and the tomato, as well as through opening itself judiciously to non-vegetable ingredients – has given rise to many mouth-watering ideas. Accordingly, for this book, Academia Barilla, has selected 50 recipes for unique salad ideas.

The majority of these recipes belong to Italian cuisine, whether for their creative inspiration and use of Mediterranean products or for their regional typicality: the famous Insalata Caprese – mozzarella, tomato and basil; the extraordinary Rabbit Salad – characteristic of Monferrato; the humble Panzanella of Tuscan origin; the seafood salad, from the Gulf of Naples; the exuberant Ligurian Condiglione; and the fragrant orange salad, typical of Sicily. Some preparations, such as Salade Niçoise or Greek Salad, come from other culinary traditions and Academia Barilla chose them because they use, in common with Italian cuisine, the highest quality ingredients, a subtle balance between tradition and innovation and, above all, a joyous spirit. That gaiety – so typical of Italy and so indispensable – is what should burst forth from every salad, to let everyone know it is truly worthy of the name.

THE ART
OF DRESSING

According to an ancient proverb widespread in Italy, 'it takes four people to properly dress a salad: a miser to pour in the vinegar, a prodigal to add the oil, a wise man to salt it and a madman to mix it'. And if the thrifty, the brilliant and the wise could freely express themselves, perhaps they would tell the crazy person to calm down a bit... Not surprisingly, up until the end of the 17th century, the mixing of salad was handled by young maidens who were not yet betrothed: with their bare hands, they turned delicately and uniformly, without "bruising" the salad.

The Stars
Dressing is both an art and a science. First of all, the ingredients of a salad need to be allowed to show off their aromas, flavors and colors. Then, a certain order needs to be respected in the sequence of adding ingredients. Finally, the salad should be dressed just before serving, so that the vegetables do not wilt. The classic dressing consists of salt, vinegar (or lemon juice) and oil. Salt should be used in moderation and, if possible, it is best to use "whole" sea salt, which conserves all the wealth of the substances suspended in the seawater. The salt should be dissolved in the vinegar before adding it to the salad. The vinegar can be from a wide range of types: wine vinegar, white or red; traditional balsamic vinegar from Modena (the best for salads); or even vinegar made from beer, apples or milk. Then there are flavored vinegars, such as those flavored with raspberries, roses or tarragon. Vegetable oil, as well, may be produced from various sources, but the ideal for uncooked use is olive oil, preferably extra-virgin, with a delicate flavor, so that it does not overwhelm the salad.

The Co-Stars
To flavour or to add a particular touch to the trio of salt-vinegar-oil, you can add spices and aromas from

the garden (pepper – white, black, green or pink – chives, mint, marjoram, parsley, mustard) or wild herbs from the field (pimpernel, rampion, wood sorrel, borage, hops, citronella). Anchovies, fish eggs, olives, capers or garlic can confer a more decisive flavour upon a salad; oilseeds, raw or toasted (such as sesame, almonds, walnuts, hazelnuts, pine nuts or peanuts) will make it more nutritious.

Two Sisters: Vinaigrette and Citronette
The primary dressing for salad is a vinaigrette, a French term defining an emulsion of salt, wine vinegar, extra virgin olive oil and pepper, with a basic rule of thumb calling for a ratio of three parts olive oil to one part vinegar. It is obtained by lightly mixing the various ingredients in a bowl, using a fork or whisk, while making sure that the salt is dissolved in the vinegar before adding the oil and, lastly, the freshly ground pepper (you might also try a teaspoon of mustard). To give more body and aroma to a vinaigrette, traditional balsamic vinegar of Modena can be substituted for wine vinegar, maintaining the same proportions of oil to vinegar. Citronette, a more delicate sister of vinaigrette, uses lemon juice instead of vinegar, but follows the same method and uses the same proportions. You can vary the proportions of lemon juice and oil, even making them equal proportions, and can also substitute the lemon juice, wholly or partially, for the juice of other citrus fruits. This dressing, particularly fresh and Mediterranean, is suitable for salads of new vegetables or shellfish.

Variations on a Dressing
Vinaigrette and citronette can be flavoured or enriched with other ingredients, such as cream, plain yogurt, cheeses, honey, herbs or hard-boiled eggs. This sharp Gorgonzola dressing is tasty and quick to prepare. For four servings of salad, mix 125 g (1/2 cup) of sour cream or plain yogurt with 15 ml (1 tablespoon) of lemon juice or vinegar, a pinch of salt and some freshly ground pepper. Add 50 g (1.76 ounces)

of crumbled sharp Gorgonzola and mix until it becomes a smooth dressing. Dressings with yogurt are lighter and also more aromatic when enriched with herbs. For a pleasant dressing for four salads, mix 150 ml (2/3 cup) of plain yogurt with a teaspoon of lemon juice, a pinch of salt, some freshly ground pepper, a teaspoon of powdered sweet paprika, some finely chopped chives and chopped chervil. Additionally, mayonnaise, and all the dressings based on it, is excellent for dressing salads made from fresh or cooked vegetables, as well as salads of rice, pasta, meat, or fish.

Two Successful Dressings

Created in 1924, by Italian chef Cesare Cardini, who emigrated to the United States, Caesar Salad is one of the most famous salads in the world. Originally it was a combination of romaine lettuce and cubes of stale bread, toasted in a pan with oil and garlic; it was dressed with grated Parmigiano-Reggiano, extra virgin olive oil, salt, black pepper, lemon juice and Worcestershire sauce. Later, it was enriched with additional ingredients, such as browned bacon, slices of roast chicken or shrimps and the dressing became more complex. To prepare a dressing for four, place into a blender half a peeled clove of garlic, three anchovy fillets, a teaspoon of mustard and an egg yolk. With the blender on low, drizzle in 80 ml (1/3 cup) of extra virgin olive oil, as though making a mayonnaise. Dress with a tablespoon of lemon juice (or wine vinegar), salt and freshly ground black pepper; add 50 g (1.76 ounces) of grated Parmigiano-Reggiano. Also very popular is warm bacon dressing – ideal for making vegetable salads crunchier and more flavorful. For four salads, brown 50 g (1.76 ounces) of cubed bacon over a medium heat in a pan without oil (if the bacon is lean, add a tablespoon of oil). When part of the fat has rendered and the bacon has become crunchy, remove the bacon from the pan and deglaze with 50 ml (3.50 tablespoons) of vinegar. Add a teaspoon of brown sugar and let simmer for 2-3 minutes, diluting if necessary with water. Return the bacon to the pan, correct for salt and pepper and pour the dressing, while still hot, over the salad.

14

SALADS WITH
VEGETABLES AND FRUITS

ORANGE, GRAPEFRUIT AND LEMON SALAD

INGREDIENTS FOR **4** PEOPLE

2 oranges
2 grapefruits
2 lemons
50 g (1.76 oz) valerian
50 ml (3 1/2 tbsp) extra virgin olive oil
salt, pepper

METHOD

Peel the fruit, removing not only the peels but also the white outer membranes, conserving any juice.
Slice the fruit into segments or rounds.
Whisk together the fruit juice with salt, pepper and oil.
Pour the dressing over the fruit and serve with the washed and dried valerian.

Preparation time: 20'

ASPARAGUS
SALAD

INGREDIENTS FOR 4 PEOPLE

500 g (1.1 lb) asparagus
150 g (0.33 lb) radicchio
30 g (1 oz) radishes
80 ml (1/3 cup) extra virgin olive oil
salt, pepper

METHOD

Wash the asparagus and cut to equal length. Peel the fibrous ends.
Tie into bunches and boil in salted water for 10-15 minutes with the tips upward to prevent breaking.
The asparagus should remain firm.
Drain, cool and cut lengthwise into halves and dress with salt, pepper and oil.
Wash and dry the separated radicchio leaves then cut them into thin strips and dress like the asparagus.
Arrange the asparagus and radicchio on plates then finish with thinly sliced radishes.

Preparation time: 25'
Cooking time: 15'

AVOCADO, ORANGE, MELON AND STRAWBERRY SALAD

INGREDIENTS FOR 4 PEOPLE

2 avocados
2 oranges
1/2 melon
125 g (4.38 oz) strawberries

200 g (0.44 lb) plain yogurt
a few drops of lemon juice
salt and green pepper
(or 1 tsp sugar)

METHOD

Wash, peel and halve the avocados. Remove the stones and then cube.
Wash, dry and halve the melon. Remove the seeds from one of the quarters and finely cube the flesh.
Peel the oranges (remove white membrane). Halve the wedges.
Delicately wash and dry the strawberries then cut into small pieces.
Stir everything together in a bowl.
Mix the yogurt with a few drops of lemon juice.
Season to taste with salt and green pepper, or, for a sweeter version season with sugar
to taste instead savoury or sweet it works both ways.
Pour over the yogurt dressing.

Preparation time: 20'

BEET
SALAD

INGREDIENTS FOR **4** PEOPLE

600 g (1.3 lb) cooked beets
200 g (7 oz) salad leaves
75 g (2.64 oz) slivered almonds
75 g (2.64 oz) chopped pistachios
60 ml (1/4 cup) extra virgin olive oil
20 ml (1 tbsp + 1 tsp) wine vinegar
1 garlic clove
salt, pepper

METHOD

Wrapp the beets in an aluminum foil and bake them at 200°C (400°F) for more than
one hour, until you can easily stick a fork into them. Alternatively, you can boil them.
When the beets are cool, peel and dice them into cubes of side 2 cm (0.8 in) then mix together,
in a bowl, with the oil, vinegar, salt, pepper and the whole, peeled garlic clove.
Allow to marinate for at least 15 minutes and then remove the garlic.
Arrange the washed and dried salad leaves on plates. Place the beets on top of the salad.
Sprinkle slivered almonds and chopped pistachios over the tops of the salads.

Preparation time: 10'
Marinating time: 15'

CABBAGE SALAD WITH DRIED APRICOTS AND HAZELNUTS

INGREDIENTS FOR 4 PEOPLE

300 g (0.66 lb) cabbage (round, smooth-leaved variety)
100 g (0.22 lb) dried apricots
60 g (2.1 oz) toasted hazelnuts
100 ml (1/3 cup + 1 1/2 tbsp) extra virgin olive oil
30 ml (2 tbsp) white wine vinegar
salt, pepper

METHOD

Remove the outer leaves of the cabbage, cut into thin strips then wash well and drain.
Coarsely chop the hazelnuts and cut the dried apricots into strips.
If the apricots are very dry, you can plump them in water for about 10 minutes.
Whisk together the oil, vinegar, salt and, if desired, a sprinkling of freshly ground pepper.
Pour the dressing over the cabbage and then add the apricots and hazelnut. Serve.

Preparation time: 20'

CITRUS-SCENTED CHICKPEA SALAD

INGREDIENTS FOR 4/6 PEOPLE

500 g (1.1 lb) cooked chickpeas
10 g (0.3 oz) lemon zest
10 g (0.3 oz) orange zest
10 g (0.3 oz) lime zest
75 g (2.64 oz) yellow bell pepper
50 g (1.76 oz) red bell pepper
50 g (1.76 oz) red onion
1/4 green apple
80 ml (1/3 cup) extra virgin olive oil
15 ml (1 tbsp) wine vinegar
salt, pepper

METHOD

Drain the chickpeas then rinse and drain again.
Wash and then chop the citrus zest.
Clean and finely cube the bell peppers.
Cut the onion and unpeeled apple to the same size as the finely
cubed bell peppers in the previous statement.
Combine all the ingredients and dress with the extra virgin olive oil, vinegar, salt and pepper.

Preparation time: 20'

SALAD OF SOYBEAN SPROUTS, CARROTS AND WATERMELON

INGREDIENTS FOR 4 PEOPLE

150 g (0.33 lb) soybean sprouts
200 g (0.44 lb) carrots
350 g (0.77 lb) watermelon
50 ml (3 1/2 tbsp) soy sauce
50 ml (3 1/2 tbsp) extra virgin olive oil

METHOD

Peel the carrots and cut into thin strips using a potato peeler or similar tool.
Place in ice water for about 10 minutes. Drain just before use.
Prepare the watermelon by removing the rind and seeds then cube the flesh.
Rinse the soybean sprouts and drain on a cloth with the carrot.
Mix everything together and arrange in a bowl, or in 4 individual bowls.
Dress with soy sauce and a drizzle of extra virgin olive oil. Serve.

Preparation time: 20'

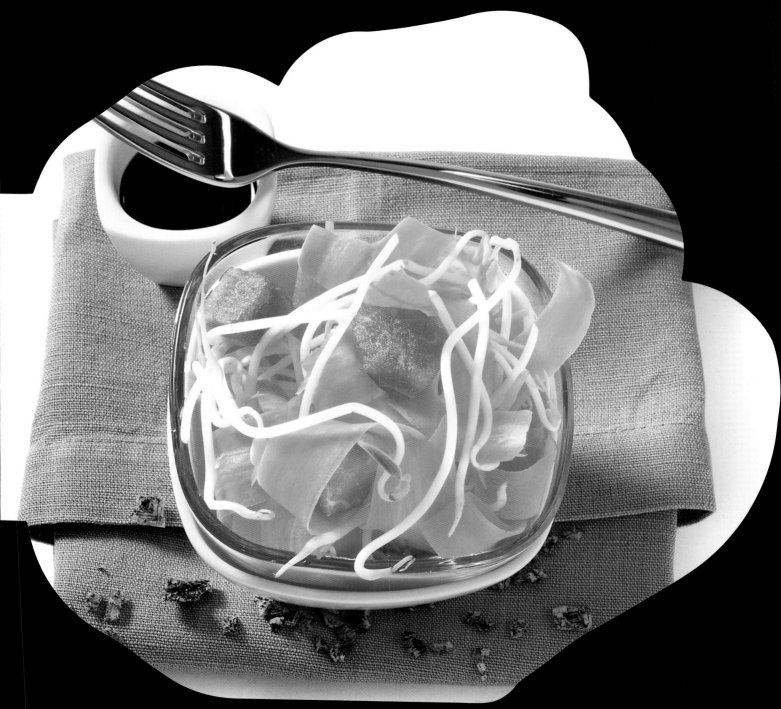

FRESH VEGETABLE
AND CORN SALAD

INGREDIENTS FOR **4** PEOPLE

500 g (1.1 lb) canned corn
300 g (0.66 lb) bell pepper
100 g (0.22 lb) cucumber
70 g (2.46 oz) celery
60 g (2.1 oz) spring onion

50 g (1.76 oz) olives
100 ml (1/3 cup + 1 1/2 tbsp)
extra virgin olive oil
20 g (0.7 oz) chopped parsley
salt, pepper

METHOD

Drain the corn and rinse under cold running water.
Wash and clean all the vegetables. Thinly slice the spring onion.
Finely cube all the other vegetables to sides of 2.5 mm (0.10 in).
Mix together the corn, vegetables, chopped olives, plenty of extra virgin olive oil,
salt and pepper to taste and a sprinkling of chopped parsley. Serve.

Preparation time: 10'

MANGO SALAD WITH
YELLOW PEPPERS AND CARROTS

INGREDIENTS FOR **4** PEOPLE

600 g (1.3 lb) mango
200 g (0.44 lb) carrots
250 g (0.55 lb) yellow bell pepper
100 ml (1/3 cup + 1 1/2 tbsp) extra virgin olive oil
1 lemon
salt

METHOD

Wash, peel and slice the mango then cut into thin strips.
Trim and wash the bell pepper and cut into strips.
Peel the carrots and cut into thin strips.
Blend together one-quarter of the mango with salt, lemon juice and the oil.
Mix the mango, carrot and bell pepper and drizzle with the dressing. Serve.

Preparation time: 20'

POTATO SALAD

INGREDIENTS FOR **4/6** PEOPLE

600 g (1.3 lb) potatoes with Yukon potatoes
For the dressing
100 ml (1/3 cup + 1 1/2 tbsp) extra virgin olive oil
30 ml (2 tbsp) wine vinegar
20 g (0.7 oz) chopped parsley
salt, pepper

or
200 ml (3/4 cup + 1 1/2 tbsp) plain yogurt
50 ml (3 1/2 tbsp) extra virgin olive oil
chives
salt, pepper

METHOD

Boil the unpeeled potatoes for about 20 minutes then allow to cool.
Peel the potatoes and slice about 0.5 cm (0.2 in) thick and place in a bowl.
Dress with extra virgin olive oil, vinegar, salt, pepper and a sprinkling of chopped parsley.
If you choose the alternative dressing then mix the yogurt with the extra virgin olive oil,
chives and a pinch of salt and pepper. Pour over the dressing. Serve.

Preparation time: 10'
Cooking time: 20'

SALAD OF CELERY ROOT, RADICCHIO AND PINEAPPLE

INGREDIENTS FOR **4** PEOPLE

300 g (0.66 lb) celery root (celeriac)
100 g (0.22 lb) radicchio
1/2 fresh pineapple
1 lemon
60 ml (1/4 cup) extra virgin olive oil
20 g (0.7 oz) chopped parsley (optional)
salt, pepper

METHOD

Wash and dry the radicchio.
Peel and cube the pineapple.
Peel and thinly slice the celery root then cut into strips and soak in cold water with the juice of the lemon.
In a blender blend a quarter of the pineapple with the extra virgin olive oil and season with salt and pepper.
Mix the celery root with the remaining pineapple.
Pour over the dressing and serve on plates over a bed of radicchio. If desired, sprinkle with chopped parsley.

Preparation time: 30'

PINK GRAPEFRUIT, SPINACH AND WALNUT SALAD

INGREDIENTS FOR 4 PEOPLE

2 pink grapefruits
2 oranges
2 lemons
200 g (7 oz) baby spinach
100 g (3.5 oz) walnut kernels
100 ml (1/3 cup + 1 1/2 tbsp) extra virgin olive oil
salt, pepper

METHOD

Wash and dry the baby spinach.
Supreme the grapefruits, oranges, and lemons
(remove the peel and the white membranes enclosing each wedge then divide into wedges).
Whisk the leftover fruit juice with the oil and a pinch of salt and pepper.
On 4 plates, arrange the spinach and the fruit wedges.
Drizzle with the dressing and sprinkle with coarsely crumbled walnuts.

Preparation time: 20'

ZUCCHINI SALAD
WITH MINT

INGREDIENTS FOR 4 PEOPLE

400 g (0.88 lb) zucchini
150 g (0.33 lb) radicchio
60 ml (1/4 cup) extra virgin olive oil
1 bunch mint
1 clove garlic
salt, pepper

METHOD

Gently warm the oil in a pan then turn off the heat then marinate the whole,
peeled garlic clove in it with a few mint leaves for about 30 minutes.
Wash and trim the radicchio and zucchini.
Cut the zucchini into thin batons and remove the inner part of the vegetable.
On a plate, arrange a bed of radicchio and the zucchini batons.
Dress with the flavoured oil, salt and pepper then garnish with mint leaves.

Preparation time: 10'
Marinating time: 30'

PINZIMONIO

INGREDIENTS FOR 4 PEOPLE

2 carrots
2 celery stalks
1/2 yellow bell pepper
1/2 red bell pepper
1/2 green bell pepper

2 green onions
1 cucumber
extra virgin olive oil
balsamic vinegar
salt, pepper

METHOD

Wash and clean the vegetables. Remove the seeds from the cucumber and bell peppers.
Cut all the vegetables into batons of equal length and place in a serving dish or 4 individual cups.
Prepare 4 small bowls containing the extra virgin olive oil.
Arrange the other condiments at the centre of the table – salt, pepper, balsamic vinegar –
which each diner can add as desired to his own bowl, for dipping the vegetables.

Preparation time: 10'

44

SALADS WITH
CHEESE AND EGGS

CAPRESE SALAD

INGREDIENTS FOR 4 PEOPLE

500 g (1.1 lb) mozzarella
600 g (1.3 lb) tomatoes
30 ml (2 tbsp) extra virgin olive oil
basil
salt

METHOD

Wash and dry the tomatoes.
Slice the mozzarella and tomatoes and lightly salt.
Gently wash and dry the basil.
Arrange the slices on a plate, alternating tomato with mozzarella and garnish with basil.
Dress the salad with extra virgin olive oil and serve.

Preparation time: 15'

GREEK SALAD

INGREDIENTS FOR 4 PEOPLE

3 tomatoes
1 red onion
2 cucumbers
200 g (0.44 lb) Feta cheese
100 ml (1/3 cup + 1 1/2 tbsp) extra virgin olive oil
50 g (1.76 oz) Greek olives
a pinch of oregano (optional)
salt

METHOD

Wash and clean the vegetables.
If desired, remove the seeds from the cucumbers.
Slice or wedge the tomatoes, slice or cube the cucumbers and slice the onion.
Cube the feta and add to the salad along with the olives.
Dress with plenty of extra virgin olive oil, salt and a sprinkling of oregano to taste.

Preparation time: 10'

WARM GOAT CHEESE SALAD

INGREDIENTS FOR 4 PEOPLE

250 g (0.55 lb) mixed salad leaves
150 g (0.33 lb) caprino (goat cheese)
200 g (0.44 lb) phyllo dough (also spelled *filo*)
100 ml (1/3 cup + 1 1/2 tbsp) extra virgin olive oil
15 ml (1 tbsp) balsamic vinegar
salt, pepper

METHOD

Cut the phyllo dough into 8 squares of side 20 cm (8 in).
Brush each with a little oil and overlap them, producing pairs.
Cut the caprino into four rounds and arrange one of the rounds at the centre
of each double square of dough.
Close the double squares into bundles.
Bake at 200°C (390°F) for about 8 minutes or fry in oil at 110°C (230°F) for 2 minutes.
Wash and dry the mixed salad leaves and arrange on plates.
Dress with extra virgin olive oil, salt, pepper and balsamic vinegar.
At the centre of each salad place one of the goat cheese bundles.

Preparation time: 15'
Cooking time: 2'-8'

ARTICHOKE SALAD WITH PARMIGIANO-REGGIANO

INGREDIENTS FOR **4** PEOPLE

4 artichokes
120 g (0.26 lb) Parmigiano-Reggiano
2 lemons
20 g (0.7 oz) chopped parsley
50 ml (3 1/2 tbsp) extra virgin olive oil (preferably Ligurian)
salt, pepper

METHOD

Trim the artichokes, remove the outer leaves and thorns and clean the stems.
Immerse the artichokes in a container of water and lemon juice for 15 minutes.
Flake the Parmigiano-Reggiano.
Whisk the lemon juice, extra virgin olive oil, a pinch of salt and some freshly ground pepper.
Cut the artichokes in half and remove any stringy filaments then slice thinly
and drizzle with the dressing.
Arrange the artichoke slices at the centre of the plate and garnish with flakes
of Parmigiano-Reggiano, chopped parsley, and a drizzle of extra virgin olive oil.

Preparation time: 20'

ASSORTED
CHEESE SALAD

INGREDIENTS FOR 4/6 PEOPLE

100 g (0.22 lb) Gruyere cheese
100 g (0.22 lb) Provolone cheese
100 g (0.22 lb) Caciocavallo cheese
100 g (0.22 lb) Asiago cheese
100 g (0.22 lb) radicchio
80 g (2.8 oz) celery
50 g (1.76 oz) radishes
10 g (0.3 oz) chives

For the dressing
80 g (2.8 oz) mayonnaise
125 g (4.38 oz) plain yogurt
salt

or
80 ml (1/3 cup) extra virgin olive oil
25 ml (1 1/2 tbsp) balsamic vinegar
salt

METHOD

Remove the rind from the cheeses before cutting into thin batons.
Clean and wash the celery, radicchio and radishes then slice them into strips.
Wash and finely chop the chives.
In a bowl, mix everything together and pour over the mayonnaise, yogurt and pinch
of salt dressing or, alternatively, the oil, salt and balsamic vinegar dressing.

Preparation time: 20'

PECORINO SALAD WITH FAVA BEANS AND PARMA HAM

INGREDIENTS FOR 4 PEOPLE

600 g (1.3 lb) fresh fava beans
200 g (0.44 lb) sliced Parma ham (prosciutto di Parma)
200 g (0.44 lb) medium-aged pecorino cheese
100 g (0.22 lb) mixed salad leaves
15 ml (1 tbsp) wine vinegar
60 ml (1/4 cup) extra virgin olive oil
salt

METHOD

Shell the beans and cook in boiling salted water for about 10 minutes. Drain, cool and remove the skins.
Put into a bowl and season with a drizzle of extra virgin olive oil and a pinch of salt.
Thinly slice the pecorino using a potato peeler or similar tool.
Dress the mixed salad leaves with the remaining extra virgin olive oil, a pinch of salt and the vinegar.
Add the fava beans, the pecorino and the slices of Parma ham and serve.

Preparation time: 20'
Cooking time: 10'

PEAR SALAD WITH GORGONZOLA AND WALNUTS

INGREDIENTS FOR 4 PEOPLE

2 pears
120 g (0.26 lb) Gorgonzola cheese
200 g (0.44 lb) red or green leaf lettuce
50 g (1.76 oz) walnut kernels
100 ml (1/3 cup + 1 1/2 tbsp) extra virgin olive oil
salt, pepper

METHOD

Trim and wash the salad.
Slice or cube the washed pears, leaving the skin on if you wish.
On plates, arrange the salad leaves and, over this, add the pears and hand-broken Gorgonzola chunks.
Sprinkle with crushed walnuts and season with salt, pepper and extra virgin olive oil.
As an alternative, you can halve the pears, scoop out the flesh, leaving the empty shells and dice
the pear flesh, mix with the Gorgonzola and fill the pear halves with the mixture,
arranging one pear-half on top of each salad.

Preparation time: 15'

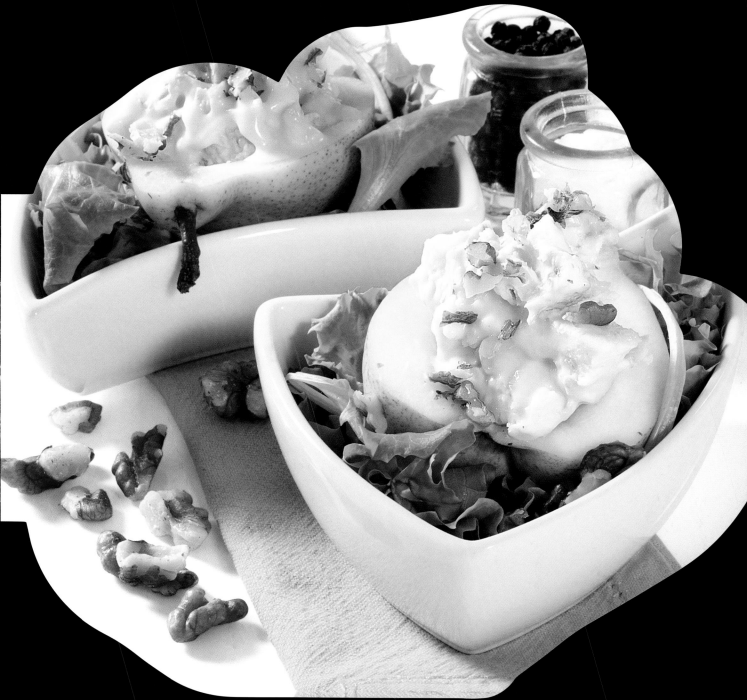

ARUGULA SALAD WITH PARMIGIANO-REGGIANO

INGREDIENTS FOR 4 PEOPLE

200 g (0.44 lb) arugula
150 g (0.33 lb) Parmigiano-Reggiano
50 ml (3 1/2 tbsp) extra virgin olive oil
15 ml (1 tbsp) balsamic vinegar
salt, pepper

METHOD

Wash and dry the arugula.
Whisk the balsamic vinegar, salt, pepper and oil in a small bowl.
Thinly slice the Parmigiano-Reggiano with a potato peeler or similar tool.
On plates, arrange the arugula and sprinkle over the Parmigiano-Reggiano.
Drizzle with the dressing.

Preparation time: 15'

SALADE NIÇOISE

INGREDIENTS FOR **4** PEOPLE

4 eggs
400 g (0.88 lb) potatoes
100 g (0.22 lb) lettuce
300 g (0.66 lb) green beans
400 g (0.88 lb) tomatoes
300 g (0.66 lb) tuna (in oil)

50 g (1.76 oz) olives
4 salted anchovies
100 ml (1/3 cup + 1 1/2 tbsp) extra virgin olive oil
1 tsp mustard
25 ml (1 1/2 tbsp) red wine vinegar
salt, pepper

METHOD

Place the eggs in a sauce pan and cover with water. Bring to boil. Allow to boil for 8-10 minutes. Rinse the eggs under cold running water to stop the cooking. Peel the eggs and cut into wedges. Wash the potatoes and boil in plenty of salted water, leaving the skins on then drain, cool, peel and cut into 1 cm (0.4 in) slices. Dress with salt, pepper, a dash of vinegar and a drizzle of olive oil.
Trim and boil the green beans in salted water then drain and cool immediately in iced water to stop the cooking and retain the colour. Wash the tomatoes and cut into wedges. Wash and dry the lettuce.
Drain the tuna and flake into large chunks then rinse and fillet the anchovies. For the vinaigrette dressing, whisk the remaining oil with the red wine vinegar, a one teaspoon of mustard, salt and pepper.
On individual plates, or in a salad bowl, arrange a bed of lettuce and, over this, arrange the potatoes and green beans. Surround these with the wedges of hard-boiled eggs, alternating with tomato wedges and chunks of tuna.
Garnish with anchovy fillets and olives then dress with the vinaigrette.

Preparation time: 1 h
Cooking time: 20'

64

SALADS WITH
MEAT AND FISH

CONDIGLIONE

INGREDIENTS FOR **4** PEOPLE

600 g (1.3 lb) tomatoes, not too ripe
200 g (0.44 lb) yellow bell pepper
200 g (0.44 lb) cucumber
150 g (0.33 lb) red onion
50 g (1.76 oz) black olives from Liguria
40 g (1.41 oz) salted anchovy fillets

50 ml (3 1/2 tbsp) extra virgin olive
oil from Liguria
15 ml (1 tbsp) wine vinegar
4-5 basil leaves
1 clove garlic
salt

METHOD

Rinse the anchovies under running water and remove the bones.
Clean and wash all the vegetables, finely slice the onion, cut the bell pepper
into strips and slice the cucumber.
Slice or wedge the tomatoes.
Place the cut vegetables in a salad bowl. Add the olives, the halved anchovy fillets,
the hand-torn basil and the whole, peeled garlic (sliced if you prefer a stronger flavour).
Marinate in salt, vinegar and oil for about 10 minutes, then serve.

Preparation time: 20'
Marinating time: 10'

RABBIT SALAD WITH LAMB'S LETTUCE

INGREDIENTS FOR 4 PEOPLE

1/2 rabbit (approx. 600 g, or 1.3 lb)
150 g (0.33 lb) onions
100 g (0.22 lb) carrots
70 g (2.46 oz) celery
150 g (0.33 lb) lamb's lettuce (also called
Lewiston cornsalad or mâche)
200 ml (3/4 cups + 1 1/2 tbsp) extra virgin olive oil

5 juniper berries
5 peppercorns
1 clove
1 bay leaf
1 sprig sage
1 clove garlic
salt

METHOD

In a large pot, prepare a stock by adding the onions, carrots, celery, cloves, 3 juniper berries
and the peppercorns to some water. Boil for 15 minutes, then add some salt and the rabbit.
Simmer over low heat for one hour.
Let the rabbit cool in its stock, then drain the rabbit and remove the flesh, using your hands,
reducing it to strips.
Put the rabbit meat into a bowl along with the sage, bay leaf, 2 juniper berries
and the clove of garlic, peeled and whole.
Cover completely with the oil and leave to rest in the refrigerator until the next day
(it will keep well for 3-4 days).
Clean and wash the lamb's lettuce. Arrange some lamb's lettuce on each plate and add strips of meat.

Preparation time: 30'
Cooking time: 1 h Resting time: 24 h

ENDIVE AND PROSCIUTTO SALAD

INGREDIENTS FOR **4** PEOPLE

100 g (0.22 lb) Belgian endive
50 g (1.76 oz) arugula
100 g (0.22 lb) iceberg lettuce
200 g (0.44 lb) prosciutto crudo (Parma ham)
60 ml (1/4 cup) extra virgin olive oil
15 ml (1 tbsp) balsamic vinegar
1 tsp poppy seeds
salt

METHOD

Remove the leaves from the endive; wash and dry. Cut half of the leaves into thin strips.
Wash and dry the arugula and the iceberg lettuce.
Cut the iceberg lettuce into thin strips, as for the endive.
Arrange the endive leaves on plates and, on top of these, place the strips of arugula
and iceberg lettuce, mixed together. Now add the prosciutto in slices or in strips.
Sprinkle with a pinch of poppy seeds and dress to taste with extra virgin olive oil,
salt and balsamic vinegar.

Preparation time: 20'

APPLE, CHICKEN AND
TOASTED FOCACCIA SALAD

INGREDIENTS FOR 4 PEOPLE

2 green apples
200 g (0.44 lb) radicchio
300 g (0.66 lb) chicken breast
100 g (0.22 lb) focaccia
20 g (0.7 oz) sliced almonds
100 ml (1/3 cup + 1 1/2 tbsp) extra virgin olive oil
20 ml (1 tbsp + 1 tsp) vinegar
salt, pepper

METHOD

Wash and dry the radicchio, then slice thinly.
Wash and dry the apples and, without peeling them, cut them into cubes.
Dress the chicken breast with salt, pepper and a drizzle of extra virgin olive oil
then bake at 180°C (350°F)
for 18-20 minutes (alternatively, you can grill it).
After baking let it cool and then cut into cubes.
Cut the focaccia into cubes and toast in the oven for 5 minutes.
On individual plates, arrange a bed of radicchio dressed with oil, vinegar, salt and pepper.
Add the apples, chicken and focaccia.

Preparation time: 30'
Cooking time: 20'

CHICKEN SALAD
WITH BALSAMIC VINEGAR
AND PINE NUTS

INGREDIENTS FOR **4** PEOPLE

400 g (0.88 lb) chicken breast
50 g (1.76 oz) pine nuts
100 g (0.22 lb) rocket (or arugula)
200 ml (3/4 cup + 1 1/2 tbsp)
balsamic vinegar
350 ml (1 1/2 cups) water

100 ml (1/3 cup + 1 1/2 tbsp) extra virgin olive oil
2 sprigs of sage
2 sprigs of rosemary
1 bay leaf
1 clove garlic
salt, pepper

METHOD

Clean and wash the arugula. Rinse the rosemary, the bay leaf and the sage and peel the clove of garlic.
Chop half of the herbs.
Clean and separate the chicken breasts.
In a saucepan, over medium heat, put 150 ml (0.66 cup) of balsamic vinegar, a little salt, the unchopped herbs and cover with water. Bring to a boil and add the chicken breasts. Cook for about 20 minutes.
When cooked, let the chicken breasts cool in the liquid.
Slice the chicken breast and allow to marinate with oil and the chopped herbs for about 15 minutes.
In a skillet, over medium heat, toast the pine nuts, taking care not to let them become too dark.
In a bowl, emulsify the remaining balsamic vinegar with the oil and a pinch of salt and pepper.
At the centre of each plate, arrange a little arugula, dress with vinegar and oil dressing and lay slices of chicken on top. Sprinkle with toasted pine nuts.
Finish with a few more drops of the dressing to season the rocket.

Preparation time: 15'
Cooking time: 20'

OCTOPUS SALAD WITH CITRUS FRUITS

INGREDIENTS FOR **4** PEOPLE

500 g (1.1 lb) octopus
150 g (0.33 lb) onion
150 g (0.33 lb) curly endive
100 g (0.22 lb) carrots
70 g (2.46 oz) celery

1 orange
1 lemon
1 grapefruit
80 ml (1/3 cup) extra virgin olive oil
salt, pepper

METHOD

In a large enough pot, prepare a stock with water and the onion, carrot and celery. Allow to boil for 15 minutes, then add salt and the octopus, making sure to dip it quickly 3 times before immersing it to ensure it remains tender. Cook for one hour or until it becomes tender (test it with a knife).
After cooking, turn off the heat, cover the pot with a lid and let it rest in its own water for an hour.
Drain and cut into pieces.
Peel the citrus fruits, removing not only the peel but also the white membrane covering the wedges (the wedges will be part of the salad). To do this, pass a knife between the wedge and the membrane dividing it from the others.
Using your hands, squeeze any remaining juice into a bowl.
Add the oil and a pinch of salt and pepper to the juice and mix well with a whisk to obtain the salad dressing.
On a serving plate, arrange the salad, washed and dried, the citrus fruit wedges and sliced octopus.
Dress the salad.

Preparation time: 30'
Cooking time: 1 h

MONKFISH AND TOMATO SALAD

INGREDIENTS FOR 4 PEOPLE

500 g (1.1 lb) of cleaned monkfish fillets
500 g (1.1 lb) tomatoes
20 g (0.7 oz) salted capers
100 ml (1/3 cup + 1 1/2 tbsp) extra virgin olive oil
salt, pepper

METHOD

Season the monkfish fillets with salt and pepper and set on a baking pan greased with a little oil.
Bake at 160°C (320°F) for about 8-10 minutes.
After cooking, allow to cool before cutting into slices.
Using a blender, blend the salted capers with the oil to obtain a caper sauce.
Wash the tomatoes and slice into rounds.
On individual plates, arrange the tomatoes, alternating with slices of monkfish.
Dress with salt and oil.
Drizzle a little caper sauce over the salad.

Preparation time: 25'
Cooking time: 10'

SMOKED SALMON AND FENNEL SALAD

INGREDIENTS FOR **4** PEOPLE

450 g (1 lb) fennel
200 g (0.44 lb) smoked salmon
2 lemons
100 ml (1/3 cup + 1 1/2 tbsp) extra virgin olive oil
salt, pepper

METHOD

Slice the salmon and arrange on a plate. Drizzle the juice of 1 lemon over it and allow
to marinate for about 10 minutes.
Meanwhile, trim the fennel (saving the green part for salad decoration) and slice as finely as possible.
Wash, drain thoroughly and set aside in a container.
In a bowl, whisk the juice of the other lemon, the oil, salt and pepper
then use part of this to dress the fennel.
Arrange the fennel salad on plates and cover with slices of salmon.
Drizzle with the remaining dressing and decorate with the fennel greens.

Preparation time: 30'

TUNA SALAD WITH BEANS

INGREDIENTS FOR 4 PEOPLE

200 g (0.44 lb) baby lettuce
150 g (0.33 lb) dried cannellini beans
150 g (0.33 lb) canned tuna (in oil)
50 g (1.76 oz) red bell pepper
200 g (0.44 lb) red onion
100 ml (1/3 cup + 1 1/2 tbsp) extra virgin olive oil
salt, pepper

METHOD

Soak the beans in cold water for at least 12 hours.
Boil in unsalted water until tender (about an hour). Add salt only after cooking. Allow to cool.
Wash and dry the baby lettuce. Wash and clean the bell pepper, then slice thinly.
Arrange a bed of lettuce on individual plates and, on top of this, arrange the onions, cut into rings,
the beans, drained and seasoned with a drizzle of extra virgin olive oil and salt, and the tuna,
drained of its oil.
Garnish with thin strips of bell pepper and some freshly ground pepper.

Preparation time: 1 h 30'
Soaking time: 12 h

MIMOSA SALAD
WITH TROUT

INGREDIENTS FOR 4 PEOPLE

4 eggs
400 g (0.88 lb) potatoes
100 g (3.5 oz) mixed salad leaves
400 g (0.88 lb) trout fillet

40 g (1.41 oz) walnut kernels
100 ml (1/3 cup + 1 1/2 tbsp) extra virgin olive oil
1 lemon
salt, pepper

METHOD

Place the eggs in a saucepan and cover with water. Bring to the boil. Allow to boil for 8 to 10 minutes.
Immediately hold the eggs under cold water, to stop the cooking and make them easier to peel.
After peeling, separate the yolks from the whites (which are not used in this recipe).
Wash the potatoes and boil, unpeeled, in plenty of salted water. Drain, cool, peel and cut into wedges, about 1/2 cm (0.2 inches) thick.
Wash and dry the mixed salad leaves.
Carefully remove any bones from the trout fillets. Season with pepper and arrange on a baking tray greased with a little oil.
Bake at 180°C (350°F) for about 8-10 minutes.
After cooking, allow to cool and remove the skin.
On individual plates, arrange a bed of mixed salad leaves dressed salt, oil and lemon juice. Beside this, arrange the sliced potatoes and trout. Dress everything with oil, lemon juice and a pinch of salt.
Pass the hard-boiled egg yolks through a sieve and sprinkle over the salad along with a few walnut kernels.

Preparation time: 50'
Cooking time: 10'

VEAL SALAD WITH HONEY-SESAME DRESSING

INGREDIENTS FOR **4** PEOPLE

150 g (0.33 lb) celery
150 g (0.33 lb) carrots
400 g (0.88 lb) roast veal
30 g (1 oz) radishes
20 g (0.7 oz) chopped parsley
80 ml (1/3 cup) extra virgin olive oil
40 g (1.41 oz) honey
25 g (0.88 oz) mustard
10 g (0.3 oz) sesame seeds
salt, pepper

METHOD

Wash and dry the celery. Slice thinly.
Peel the carrots and slice into thin strips.
Trim and wash the radishes and slice into thin rounds.
Now cut the cold roast veal into pieces.
Mix the meat with the vegetables, dress with salt, pepper and half of the oil and chopped parsley.
In a pan, over medium heat, toast the sesame seeds, then allow them to cool.
Blender together the sesame seeds, honey, mustard and the remaining oil. Add salt to taste.
On a plate arrange the salad and drizzle with the honey-sesame dressing.

Preparation time: 20'

MIXED SALAD GREENS WITH SPECK AND RASPBERRIES

INGREDIENTS FOR **4** PEOPLE

200 g (0.44 lb) mixed salad greens
150 g (0.33 lb) speck
60 g (2.1 oz) raspberries
50 ml (3 1/2 tbsp) extra virgin olive oil
15 ml (1 tbsp) raspberry-flavoured vinegar
salt, pepper

METHOD

Wash and dry the mixed salad leaves.
Thinly slice half of the speck and slice the rest into 3 mm (0.10 in) thick batons.
Arrange the mixed salad leaves on plates with the sticks of speck mixed in.
Surround with the thin slices of speck and decorate with the gently rinsed and dried raspberries.
In a bowl, whisk the oil, vinegar, salt and pepper then use to dress the salad.

Preparation time: 15′

PANZANELLA

INGREDIENTS FOR **4/6** PEOPLE

1 kg (2.2 lb) stale Tuscan bread
30 g (1 oz) anchovy fillets
200 g (0.44 lb) tomatoes
120 g (0.26 lb) cucumbers
(without the seeds)
150 g (0.33 lb) red onions
250 g (0.55 lb) sweet bell peppers
1 clove garlic, minced

1 tbsp capers, salt removed
(or caper fruits)
1 bunch basil
15 ml (1 tbsp) red wine vinegar
80 ml (1/3 cup) extra virgin olive oil
(preferably Tuscan)
3 g (1/2 tsp) salt
black pepper

METHOD

Cut the bread into 2 cm (0.4 in) cubes without removing the crust.
Cut the tomatoes into similar sizes.
Peel the garlic and mince with the anchovies and the capers then place the mixture in a large bowl.
Add the salt, freshly ground pepper, vinegar and oil then mix well.
Finally, add the bread, the basil and all the washed, dried and cubed vegetables.
Stir well and, if necessary, add salt and pepper to taste.

Preparation time: 15'

OCTOPUS SALAD
WITH POTATOES

INGREDIENTS FOR **4** PEOPLE

500 g (1.1 lb) octopus
500 g (1.1 lb) potatoes
1 onion
1 carrot
3 stalks of celery

80 g (2.8 oz) black olives
100 ml (1/3 cup + 1 1/2 tbsp) extra virgin olive oil
1 lemon
1 tbsp chopped parsley
salt, pepper

METHOD

Bring a pan of salted water to the boil. When it begins to boil, add the onion, carrot and one stalk of trimmed and washed celery. Allow to cook for five minutes. Quickly dip the octopus into the boiling water 3 times before immersing it to ensure it remains tender.
Cook for one hour or until soft, test it with a knife. Once the octopus is cooked, turn off the heat, cover the pot with a lid and allow to cool in its own water for one hour.
Meanwhile, peel the potatoes, wash and boil in salted water for about 15-20 minutes.
Drain, allow to cool and cut into wedges or cubes.
Wash and dry the remaining celery stalks and cut into pieces.
Juice the lemon. In a bowl, whisk the lemon juice with the oil, salt and pepper.
Once the octopus has cooled, drain and cut into pieces.
Prepare the salad by combining the potatoes, celery, black olives and octopus.
Pour over the dressing and sprinkle with chopped parsley.
Drizzle with the remaining extra virgin olive oil and serve.

Preparation time: 15'
Cooling time: 1 h Cooking time: 1 h

94

SALADS WITH
PASTA AND GRAINS

GRAIN SALAD WITH HERBS AND VEGETABLES

INGREDIENTS FOR **4/6** PEOPLE

70 g (2.46 oz) rice
70 g (2.46 oz) barley
70 g (2.46 oz) spelt
60 ml (1/4 cup) extra virgin olive oil
50 g (1.76 oz) celery
100 g (0.22 lb) leeks
200 g (0.44 lb) eggplant
100 g (0.22 lb) zucchini

100 g (0.22 lb) red bell pepper
100 g (0.22 lb) yellow bell pepper
150 g (0.33 lb) carrots
2 sprigs thyme
2 sprigs marjoram
2 sprigs sage
2 sprigs rosemary
salt

METHOD

Boil separately in salted water the rice, barley and spelt (for an alternative, to speed preparation, you can use a mix of precooked grains). Drain while still al dente and let cool, spreading out in a pan and stirring occasionally.
Meanwhile, wash and drain the vegetables. Dice the carrots, celery, bell peppers and zucchini.
Cube the eggplant, lightly salt it and allow to drain in a colander for about 30 minutes.
Slice the white part of the leek. Wash and dry and chop the herbs.
In a pan, sauté each of the vegetables separately with a little oil and the chopped herbs, until crisp-tender.
Season with salt then add to a bowl with the grains.
Dress with the remaining extra virgin olive oil, and add salt to taste.

Preparation time: 15'
Cooking time: 45'

MARGHERITA-STYLE
PASTA SALAD

INGREDIENTS FOR **4** PEOPLE

320 g (0.7 lb) shell-shaped pasta
250 g (0.55 lb) mozzarella
2 tomatoes
4-5 basil leaves
80 ml (1/3 cup) extra virgin olive oil
salt

METHOD

Boil the pasta in plenty of salted water. While still quite al dente, stop the cooking and
cool the pasta by quickly rinsing under cold running water and then drain carefully.
Put the pasta in a large bowl and toss with a drizzle of olive oil so that it does not stick together.
Wash the tomatoes and remove their seeds. Cut the tomatoes and the mozzarella into cubes
of side 1 cm (0.4 inches) and mix together with the pasta in the large bowl.
Dress with a pinch of salt, hand-torn basil and the extra virgin olive oil.
Serve.

Preparation time: 15'
Cooking time: 8'

VEGETARIAN COUSCOUS SALAD

INGREDIENTS FOR 4 PEOPLE

300 g (0.66 lb) cooked couscous
100 g (0.22 lb) red onion
50 g (1.76 oz) peas
50 g (1.76 oz) yellow bell pepper
100 g (0.22 lb) carrots

100 g (0.22 lb) zucchini
80 ml (1/3 cup) extra virgin olive oil
300 ml (1 1/4 cup) vegetable stock (or water)
chopped parsley
salt

METHOD

Separately, bring to boil a quantity of the vegetable stock (or water) equal to the weight
of the couscous. Wet the couscous with the boiling stock and mix well with a wooden fork,
taking care that lumps do not form. Cover the pan with plastic wrap and allow to rest for about
30 minutes then carefully loosen the couscous with the wooden fork.
Meanwhile, clean and wash all the vegetables, except for the peas,
and finely cube to sides of 2-3 mm (0.1 in).
Sauté each of the vegetables separately in a little of the extra virgin olive oil,
making sure they remain crisp.
Blanch the peas.
Add all the vegetables to the couscous.
Dress with a drizzle of extra virgin olive oil. Add salt to taste and sprinkle with chopped parsley. Serve.

Preparation time: 40'

BOWTIE PASTA SALAD WITH MELON BALLS AND VEGETABLE CONFETTI

INGREDIENTS FOR **4** PEOPLE

200 g (0.44 lb) bowtie (farfalle) pasta
2 melons
100 g (0.22 lb) bell peppers
150 g (0.33 lb) zucchini

150 g (0.33 lb) carrots
50 g (1.76 oz) chopped parsley
60 ml (1/4 cup) extra virgin olive oil
salt

METHOD

Boil the pasta in plenty of salted water. While still quite al dente,
rinse the pasta under cold running water and drain carefully.
Pour into a large bowl and toss with a drizzle of olive oil to prevent it sticking together.
Wash and dry and halve the melon. Remove the seeds and make melon balls with a melon baller.
After cleaning and washing all the vegetables, finely dice and combine with the pasta.
Add the melon balls and dress with salt, extra virgin olive oil and chopped parsley.
Mix thoroughly and serve the salad in the hollow melon shells.

Preparation time: 25'
Cooking time: 12'

FUSILLI PASTA SALAD WITH ASPARAGUS AND PROSCIUTTO CRUDO

INGREDIENTS FOR **4** PEOPLE

300 g (0.66 lb) fusilli type pasta
50 g (1.76 oz) butter
130 g (4.5 oz) prosciutto crudo
200 g (0.44 lb) asparagus
50 ml (3 1/2 tbsp) extra virgin olive oil

20 g (0.7 oz) chopped parsley
1 clove garlic
zest of 1 lemon
salt, pepper

METHOD

Boil the pasta in plenty of salted water. While still quite al dente, quickly rinse under cold running water and drain carefully. Pour into a large bowl and toss with a drizzle of olive oil so it does not stick together.
Carefully wash the asparagus and remove the fibrous part. Cut into rounds, keeping the tips whole.
Place in a pan with half the butter, the garlic, peeled and whole and allow to simmer
for about 10 minutes over medium heat.
Meanwhile, cut the prosciutto into broad 8 mm (0.3 in) strips and cut the lemon zest into thin strips.
In a pan, sauté the prosciutto with the remaining butter, without letting it go dry. Moisten with a ladleful of water and add the asparagus. Season to taste with salt and pepper.
Add the asparagus and prosciutto to the pasta and mix well.
Sprinkle with a little lemon zest and chopped parsley.
Dress with extra virgin olive oil.

Preparation time: 30'
Cooking time: 13'

SARDINIAN-STYLE PASTA SALAD WITH TUNA, ZUCCHINI AND BELL PEPPERS

INGREDIENTS FOR 4 PEOPLE

300 g (0.66 lb) gnocchetti sardi (malloreddus) type pasta
400 g (0.88 lb) fresh tuna steak
300 g (0.66 lb) round zucchini (bush summer squash, globe squash)
150 g (0.33 lb) red bell pepper

150 g (0.33 lb) yellow bell pepper
100 g (0.22 lb) of fava beans
80 g (2.8 oz) peas
100 ml (1/3 cup + 1 1/2 tbsp) extra virgin olive oil
a few drops of lemon juice
salt, pepper

METHOD

Boil the pasta in plenty of salted water. While still quite al dente, quickly rinse under cold running water, then carefully drain. Pour into a large bowl and toss with a drizzle of olive oil so it does not stick together.
Separately blanch the peas and beans in salted boiling water for a couple of minutes; cool in iced water. Peel the beans.
Clean and wash the bell peppers and zucchinis, and cut them into cubes about 1 cm (0.4 inches) per side.
Sauté the vegetables with one-third of the oil, until crisp-tender then season with salt and pepper.
Cover the tuna steak with salt, pepper and a little oil, then cook on a hot griddle for a couple of minutes per side so that the tuna remains pink inside (alternatively, use a non-stick pan).
Add all the vegetables to the pasta and mix well, adding the remaining oil.
Finally, cube the tuna steak and add to the pasta mix.
Drizzle with a few drops of lemon juice to taste.

Preparation time: 30'
Cooking time: 13'

MEZZE MANICHE PASTA SALAD WITH PRAWNS, CHERRY TOMATOES AND EGGPLANT

INGREDIENTS FOR 4 PEOPLE

300 g (0.66 lb) mezze maniche type pasta
300 g (0.66 lb) eggplant
250 g (0.55 lb) cherry tomatoes
16 prawns (preferably karamote prawns)
80 g (2.8 oz) Tropea (red) onions
150 ml (2/3 cup) extra virgin olive oil

25 g (0.88 oz) salted capers
or caper fruits
20 g (0.7 oz) chopped parsley
1 clove garlic
2 sprigs thyme
salt, pepper

METHOD

Boil the pasta in plenty of salted water. While still quite al dente, quickly rinse under cold running water and drain carefully. Pour into a large bowl and toss with a drizzle of olive oil so it does not stick together.
Wash, dry and cube the eggplant. Lightly salt it and allow to drain in a colander for about 30 minutes.
Dice the onion and sauté with a drizzle of olive oil over low heat.
Wash and quarter the tomatoes. Rinse and then coarsely chop the capers.
Clean and shell the prawns. Chop the tails into pieces and sauté, with the thyme and the peeled garlic, in a little olive oil for 3-4 minutes then lightly salt.
Finally, drain the eggplant well, using paper towels to absorb any remaining moisture, then sauté in the remaining oil.
Add the eggplant, prawns, cherry tomatoes, onion, parsley and capers to the pasta, stirring well.
Dress with a drizzle of olive oil then add salt and freshly ground pepper to taste.

Preparation time: 30'
Cooking time: 13'

ORECCHIETTE PASTA SALAD WITH COD, FAVA BEANS AND OLIVES

INGREDIENTS FOR **4** PEOPLE

300 g (0.66 lb) orecchiette type pasta
200 g (0.44 lb) fava beans
250 g (0.55 lb) dried cod, soaked
50 g (1.76 oz) black olives
180 g (0.4 lb) tomatoes (ripe)

bunch of basil
100 ml (1/3 cup + 1 1/2 tbsp) extra virgin olive oil
1 clove garlic
vegetable stock
salt, pepper

METHOD

Boil the pasta in plenty of salted water. While still quite al dente,
quickly rinse under cold running water and drain carefully.
Pour into a large bowl and toss with a drizzle of olive oil so it does not stick together.
Using an immersion mixer, mix half the oil with the basil leaves, then strain the emulsion through a fine
mesh strainer. In a pan, with half the remaining oil, fry the peeled, whole garlic clove. Add the cod,
cut into chunks, add salt and pepper to taste then cook rapidly, without the fish coming apart.
If necessary, moisten with some vegetable stock.
Slit the skin of the tomato in an X and boil for 20 seconds.
Allow to cool then peel, remove the seeds and dice.
Boil the fava beans in lightly salted water. Allow to cool and then peel.
Finally, dress with the remaining oil and add salt and pepper to taste
In a bowl, mix the pasta with the fava beans, olives, tomato and cod. Add salt and pepper to taste.
Serve on plates and drizzle with the basil dressing.

Preparation time: 40'
Cooking time: 11'

WHOLE-GRAIN PASTA SALAD WITH AVOCADO, CHICKEN, CHERRY TOMATOES, AND CORN

INGREDIENTS FOR **4** PEOPLE

300 g (0.66 pounds) penne type pasta, whole grain
150 g (0.33 pounds) cherry tomatoes
150 g (0.33 pounds) chicken breast
2 avocados

20 g (0.7 ounces) chopped parsley
150 g (0.33 pounds) canned corn, plain (drained)
60 ml (1/4 cup) extra virgin olive oil
salt, pepper

METHOD

Season the chicken breast with salt, pepper, and a drizzle of extra virgin olive oil, then bake in the oven at 180°C (350°F) for 18-20 minutes (or you can grill it). Let cool then cut into cubes.
Boil the pasta in plenty of salted water. While still quite al dente, stop the cooking and cool the pasta by quickly passing under cold running water, then carefully drain.
Wash the avocados, cut into halves, remove the pit, and peel.
Using a melon baller, form small balls, or cut into cubes.
Wash the cherry tomatoes and cut into halves. Drain the corn and rinse under running water.
Mix the pasta with chicken, the cherry tomatoes, avocado, and corn.
Season with salt, extra virgin olive oil, and chopped parsley.
Mix thoroughly and serve.

Preparation time: 20'
Cooking time: 20'

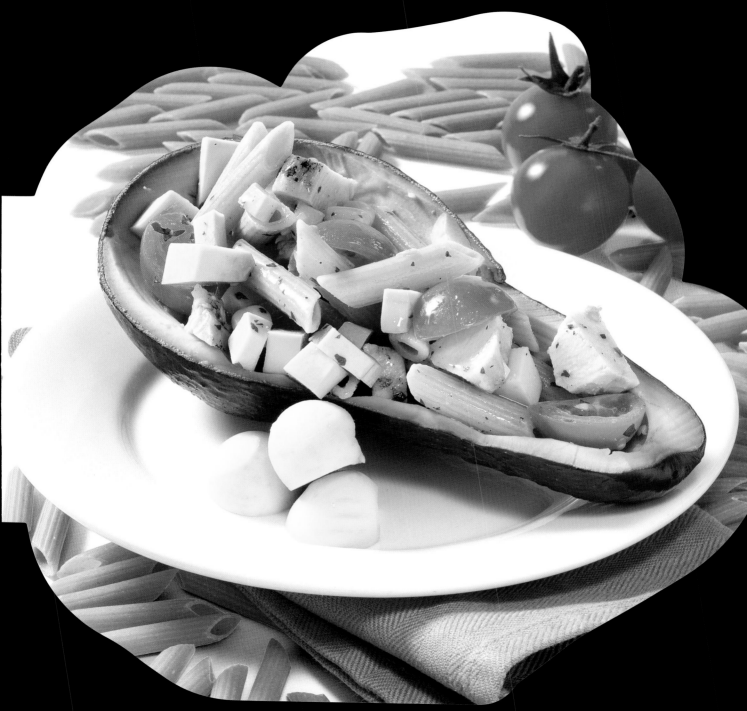

SPRING
RICE SALAD

INGREDIENTS FOR **4** PEOPLE

200 g (0.44 lb) rice
120 g (0.26 lb) peas
150 g (0.33 lb) asparagus
50 g (1.76 oz) squash blossoms
100 ml (1/3 cup + 1 1/2 tbsp) extra virgin olive oil
salt

METHOD

Add the rice to boiling salted water and cook for about 15 minutes, or for the time indicated on the package. Meanwhile, boil the peas for a couple of minutes, in boiling salted water and allow to cool in iced water. Wash the asparagus, cut them to even length, tie with string and boil for 10-15 minutes. Allow to cool then cut into pieces.
Clean and wash the squash blossoms and cut into strips.
When ready, drain the rice and quickly rinse under cold running water and place in a bowl.
Add the prepared ingredients.
Season with a pinch of salt and pour over the extra virgin olive oil.
Stir the rice salad well and serve cold.

Preparation time: 25'
Cooking time: 15'

VENUS RICE SALAD WITH CHERRY TOMATOES AND MOZZARELLA

INGREDIENTS FOR **4** PEOPLE

200 g (0.44 lb) Venus rice (Italian black long-grain rice)
50 ml (3 1/2 tbsp) extra virgin olive oil
15 g (0.53 oz) sugar
200 g (0.44 lb) cherry tomatoes
150 g (0.33 lb) mozzarelline (tiny mozzarella balls)
2-3 basil leaves
20 g (0.7 oz) chopped parsley
1 clove garlic
a pinch of dried oregano
salt, pepper

METHOD

Boil the Venus rice in salted water and drain after about 30 minutes when cooked al dente.
Meanwhile, wash and quarter the cherry tomatoes. Add salt and dress with peeled and sliced garlic,
the dried oregano, 15 ml (1 tbsp) of extra virgin olive oil, the sugar, salt and pepper.
Allow the cherry tomatoes to marinate for about 15 minutes.
Mix the rice, mozzarelline and the marinated cherry tomatoes in a bowl.
Dress with the remaining oil, parsley, the washed, dried and chopped basil and adjust
the salt and pepper to taste.

Preparation time: 40'
Cooking time: 30'

SEDANINI PASTA SALAD WITH GREEN APPLES, RAISINS AND ALMONDS

INGREDIENTS FOR 4 PEOPLE

300 g (0.66 lb) sedanini type pasta
70 g (2.46 oz) raisins
100 g (0.22 lb) slivered almonds
2 green apples

20 g (0.7 oz) chopped parsley
80 ml (1/3 cup) extra virgin olive oil
juice of 1 lemon
salt, pepper

METHOD

Boil the pasta in plenty of salted water. While still quite al dente, quickly rinse under cold running water and drain carefully. Pour into a large bowl and toss with a drizzle of olive oil so it does not stick together.
Plump the raisins by covering with water for 10-15 minutes. Drain well and squeeze gently.
Wash and slice (or cube) the apples without peeling and place in a bowl and stir in the lemon juice.
Toast the almonds in an oven for a few minutes.
Mix the pasta with the apples, raisins and toasted almonds. Drain the lemon juice from the apples and, in a bowl, whisk the juice with the salt, pepper, oil and a little of the chopped parsley then use to dress the salad.
Serve on plates and sprinkle with a few slivers of the toasted almonds.

Preparation time: 30'
Cooking time: 13'

WARM SPELT SALAD
WITH SCAMPI

INGREDIENTS FOR **4** PEOPLE

300 g (0.66 lb) pre-cooked spelt
12 scampi
100 g (0.22 lb) carrots
100 g (0.22 lb) dried tomatoes
70 g (2.46 oz) pitted black olives
80 ml (1/3 cup) extra virgin olive oil
1 tsp chopped parsley
a few basil leaves
salt

METHOD

Peel and finely cube the carrots then quickly sauté with a drizzle of olive oil until crisp-tender.
Add salt to taste.
Cut the dried tomatoes into pieces and slice the olives.
Boil the spelt in salted water then drain and place in a bowl. Add the carrots, chopped tomatoes, olives, basil and coarsely minced parsley. Finally, dress with salt and a drizzle of extra virgin olive oil.
Shell the scampi, then quick-fry for 2-3 minutes with a drizzle of olive oil. Serve with the spelt salad.

Preparation time: 30'
Cooking time: 10'

ALPHABETICAL
INDEX OF RECIPES

Apple, chicken and toasted focaccia salad — page 72
Artichoke salad with Parmigiano-Reggiano — page 52
Arugula salad with Parmigiano-Reggiano — page 60
Asparagus salad — page 18
Assorted cheese salad — page 54
Avocado, orange, melon and strawberry salad — page 20
Beet salad — page 22
Bowtie pasta salad with melon balls and vegetable confetti — page 102
Cabbage salad with dried apricots and hazelnuts — page 24
Caprese salad — page 46
Chicken salad with balsamic vinegar and pine nuts — page 74
Citrus-scented chickpea salad — page 26
Condiglione — page 66
Endive and prosciutto salad — page 70
Fresh vegetable and corn salad — page 30
Fusilli pasta salad with asparagus and prosciutto crudo — page 104
Grain salad with herbs and vegetables — page 96
Greek salad — page 48
Mango salad with yellow peppers and carrots — page 32
Margherita-style pasta salad — page 98
Mezze maniche pasta salad with prawns, cherry tomatoes and eggplant — page 108
Mimosa salad with trout — page 84
Mixed salad greens with speck and raspberries — page 88
Monkfish and tomato salad — page 78
Octopus salad with citrus fruits — page 76

Octopus salad with potatoes   page 92
Orange, grapefruit and lemon salad   page 16
Orecchiette pasta salad with cod, fava beans and olives   page 110
Panzanella   page 90
Pear salad with gorgonzola and walnuts   page 58
Pecorino salad with fava beans and Parma ham   page 56
Pink grapefruit, spinach and walnut salad   page 38
Pinzimonio   page 42
Potato salad   page 34
Rabbit salad with lamb's lettuce   page 68
Salad of celery root, radicchio and pineapple   page 36
Salad of soybean sprouts, carrots and watermelon   page 28
Salade Niçoise   page 62
Sardinian-style pasta salad with tuna, zucchini and bell peppers   page 106
Sedanini pasta salad with green apples, raisins and almonds   page 118
Smoked salmon and fennel salad   page 80
Spring rice salad   page 114
Tuna salad with beans   page 82
Veal salad with honey-sesame dressing   page 86
Vegetarian couscous salad   page 100
Venus rice salad with cherry tomatoes and mozzarella   page 116
Warm goat cheese salad   page 50
Warm spelt salad with scampi   page 120
Whole-grain pasta salad with avocado, chicken, cherry tomatoes, and corn   page 112
Zucchini salad with mint   page 40

ALPHABETICAL
INDEX OF INGREDIENTS

A
Almonds, 12, 22, 72, 118
Anchovies, 12, 13, 62, 66, 90
Apples, green, 26, 72, 118
Apricots, dried, 24
Artichokes, 9, 52
Asparagus, 18, 104, 114
Avocado, 20, 112

B
Bacon, 13
Barley, 96
Basil, 10, 46, 66, 90, 98, 110, 116, 120
Bay leaf, 68, 74
Beans, 7
Beans, cannellini, dried, 82
Beans, fava, 7, 56, 106, 110
Beans, green, 62
Beef, 7
Beets, 22
Bell peppers, 26, 30, 32, 42, 66, 90, 96, 100, 102, 106
Borage, 12
Bottarga, 7
Bread, 7, 13
Bread, focaccia, 72
Bread, Tuscan, 90
Butter, 104

C
Cabbage, 24
Caper, fruit, 90, 108
Capers, salted, 12, 78, 90, 108
Carrots, 28, 32, 42, 68, 76, 86, 92, 96, 100, 102, 120
Celery, 7, 30, 42, 54, 68, 76, 86, 92, 96
Celery root, 36
Cheese, 7, 9, 12
Cheese, Asiago, 54
Cheese, Caciocavallo, 54
Cheese, caprino, 50
Cheese, Feta, 48
Cheese, Gorgonzola, 58
Cheese, Gorgonzola, sharp, 12
Cheese, Gruyere, 54
Cheese, mozzarella, 10, 46, 98
Cheese, mozzarelline (mozzarella tidbits), 116
Cheese, Parmigiano-Reggiano, 13, 52, 60
Cheese, pecorino, 56
Cheese, Provolone, 54
Chervil, 13
Chicken breast, 7, 13, 72, 74, 112
Chickpeas, 7, 26
Chives, 12, 13, 34, 54
Citronella, 12
Citrus fruits, 12

Cloves, 68
Coriander, 7
Corn, canned, in water, 30, 112
Couscous, precooked, 100
Cream, 12
Cream, sour, 12
Crustaceans, 9, 12
Cucumbers, 30, 42, 48, 66, 90

E
Eggplant, 9, 96, 108
Eggs, 12, 13, 62, 84
Eggs, fish, 12
Endive, Belgian, 70
Endive, curly, 76

F
Fennel, 80
Fish, 6, 7, 9, 13
Flowers, 6, 8
Fruit, 6, 7, 8

G
Garlic, 12, 13, 22, 40, 66, 68, 74, 90, 104, 108, 110, 116
Grapefruit, 16, 38, 76

H
Hazelnuts, 12, 24
Herbs, 6, 8, 12

Honey, 12, 86
Hops, 12

J
Juniper berries, 68

L
Lambs lettuce (corn salad), 68, 112, 116, 118, 120
Leeks, 6, 7, 96
Lemon, 6, 7, 11, 12, 13, 16, 20, 26, 32, 36, 38, 52, 76, 80, 84, 92, 104, 106, 118
Lettuce, 6, 7, 62
Lettuce, baby, 6, 82
Lettuce, iceberg, 70
Lettuce, red or green leaf, 58
Lettuce, romaine, 13
Lime, 26

M
Mallow, 6
Mango, 32
Marjoram, 12, 96
Mayonnaise, 13, 54
Meat, 6, 7, 9, 13
Melon, 20, 102
Mint, 6, 7, 12, 40
Mixed salad greens, 22, 50, 56, 84, 88

Monkfish, filet of, 78
Mustard, 12, 13, 62, 86

O
Octopus, 76, 92
Oil, 6, 7, 11, 13
Oil, basil flavoured, 11
Oil, chilli pepper, 11
Oil, olive, extra virgin, 11, 12, 13, 16, 18, 22, 24, 26, 28, 30, 32, 34, 36, 38, 40, 42, 46, 48, 50, 52, 54, 56, 58, 60, 62, 66, 68, 70, 72, 74, 76, 78, 80, 82, 84, 86, 88, 90, 92, 96, 98, 100, 102, 104, 106, 108, 110, 112, 114, 116, 118, 120
Oil, wild fennel flavoured, 11
Olives, 12, 30, 62
Olives, Greek, 48, 92, 110, 66, 120
Onions, 68, 76, 92
Onions, green, 30, 42
Onions, red, 26, 48, 66, 82, 90, 100
Onions, Tropea, 108
Oranges, 10, 16, 20, 26, 38, 76
Oregano, 48
Oregano, dried, 116

P
Paprika, powdered, sweet, 13
Parma ham, 9, 56, 70, 104

Parsley, 12, 30, 34, 36, 52, 86, 92, 100, 102, 104, 108, 112, 116, 118, 120
Pasta, 6, 13
Pasta, farfalle (bowtie), 102
Pasta, fusilli, 104
Pasta, gnocchetti sardi, 106
Pasta, mezze maniche, 108
Pasta, orecchiette, 110
Pasta, sedanini, 118
Pasta, shell, 98
Pasta, penne, whole grain, 112
Peanuts, 12
Pears, 58
Peas, 100, 106, 114
Pepper, 12, 13, 16, 18, 22, 24, 26, 30, 34, 36, 38, 40, 42, 50, 52, 58, 60, 62, 68, 72, 74, 76, 78, 80, 82, 84, 86, 88, 92, 104, 106, 108, 110, 116, 118
Pepper, black, 12, 13, 90
Pepper, green, 12, 20
Pepper, pink, 12
Pepper, white, 12
Phyllo dough, 50
Pimpernel, 12
Pine nuts, 12, 74
Pineapple, 36
Pistachios, chopped, 22
Poppy seeds, 70
Potatoes, 9, 62, 84, 92

125

Potatoes, yellow flesh, 34
Prawns, 108

R
Rabbit, 10, 68
Radicchio, 18, 36, 40, 54, 72
Radishes, 18, 54, 86
Raisins, 118
Rampion, 12
Raspberries, 88
Rice, 6, 13, 96, 114
Rice, Venus, 116
Rocket, 7, 60, 70, 74
Rosemary, 74, 96
Rue, 7

S
Sage, 68, 74, 96
Salmon, smoked, 80
Salt cod, soaked, 110
Savory, 7
Scampi, 120
Seeds, oil, 8, 12
Sesame seeds, 12, 86
Shrimps, 13

Soy sauce, 28
Soy sprouts, 28
Speck, 88
Spelt, 9, 96, 120
Spinach, baby, 38
Squash blossoms, 114
Strawberries, 20
Stock, vegetable, 100, 110
Sugar, 20, 116
Sugar, cane, 13

T
Thyme, 7, 96, 108
Tomatoes, 9, 10, 46, 48, 62, 66,
    78, 90, 98, 110
Tomatoes cherry, 108, 112, 116
Tomatoes dried, 120
Trout, filet of, 84
Tuna, canned, in oil, 62, 82
Tuna, fresh, 106

V
Valerian, 16
Veal, roast, 86
Vegetables, 6, 7, 8, 9, 13, 14

Vinegar, 6, 7, 9, 11, 12, 13, 72
Vinegar, apple cider, 11
Vinegar, balsamic, 11, 12, 42, 50,
    54, 60, 70, 74
Vinegar, beer, 11
Vinegar, milk, 11
Vinegar, raspberry-flavoured, 11,
    88
Vinegar, rose-flavoured, 11
Vinegar, tarragon-flavoured, 11
Vinegar, wine, 11, 12, 13, 22, 24,
    26, 34, 56, 62, 66, 90

W
Walnut kernels, 7, 12, 38, 58,
    84
Watermelon, 28
Wood sorrel, 12
Worcestershire sauce, 13

Y
Yogurt, 12, 13, 20, 34, 54

Z
Zucchini, 40, 96, 100, 102, 106

All photographs are the property of Academia Barilla except:

©123RF: pages cover, 2, 4, 5, 7, 8, 10, 123, 125, 126, 128, timer image
©iStockphoto: pages 13, 14-15, 42-43, 64-65, 88-89

ACADEMIA BARILLA

AMBASSADOR OF ITALIAN GASTRONOMY THROUGHOUT THE WORLD

In the heart of Parma, one of the most distinguished capitals of Italian cuisine, is the Barilla Center. Set in the grounds of the former Barilla pasta factory, this modern architectural complex is the home of Academia Barilla. This was founded in 2004 to promote the art of Italian cuisine, protecting the regional gastronomic heritage and safeguarding it from imitations and counterfeits, while encouraging the great traditions of the Italian restaurant industry. Academia Barilla is also a center of great professionalism and talent that is exceptional in the world of cooking. It organizes cooking classes for culinary enthusiasts, it provides services for those involved in the restaurant industry, and it offers products of the highest quality. In 2007, Academia Barilla was awarded the "Premio Impresa-Cultura" for its campaigns promoting the culture and creativity of Italian gastronomy throughout the world. The center was designed to meet the training requirements of the world of food and it is equipped with all the multimedia facilities necessary for organizing major events. The remarkable gastronomic auditorium is surrounded by a restaurant, a laboratory for sensory analysis, and various teaching rooms equipped with the most modern technology. The Gastronomic Library contains over 10,000 books and a remarkable collection of historic menus as well as prints related to culinary subjects. The vast cultural heritage of the library can be consulted on the internet which provides access to hundreds of digitized historic texts.

This avant-garde approach and the presence of a team of internationally famous experts enables Academia Barilla to offer a wide range of courses, meeting the needs of both restaurant chefs and amateur food lovers. In addition, Academia Barilla arranges cultural events and activities aiming to develop the art of cooking, supervised by experts, chefs, and food critics, that are open to the public. It also organizes the "Academia Barilla Film Award", for short films devoted to Italy's culinary traditions.

www.academiabarilla.com

WHITE STAR PUBLISHERS

WS White Star Publishers® is a registered trademark
property of White Star s.r.l.

© 2013 White Star s.r.l.
Piazzale Luigi Cadorna, 6
20123 Milan, Italy
www.whitestar.it

Translation: John Venerella

ISBN 978-88-544-0727-5
4 5 6   22 21 20 19 18

Printed in China